The Little Rijksmuseum

Amsterdam · Antwerpen
Em. Querido's Uitgeverij BV
2013

eyes

chicken

sunflower

girl

basket

doll

house

Johannes Vermeer
View of Houses in Delft, known as 'The Little Street', c. 1658
(trimmed)
Oil on canvas, 54.3 x 44 cm

letter

[18]

bow

pipe

Matthijs Maris
Portrait of Ludwig Casimir Sierig, Painter, 1856
(trimmed)
Oil on paper on cardboard, 26.2 x 19.7 cm

deer

asparagus

Adriaen Coorte
Still Life with Asparagus, 1697
(trimmed)
Oil on paper on panel, 25 x 20.5 cm

parasol

Jan Brandes
Slave with an Indonesian Parasol (Pajoeng), Child and Dog, c. 1779-85
(trimmed)
Pencil and watercolour, 19.5 x 15.5 cm

[28]

drum

necklace

Anonymous
Woman with a Peacock, c. 1795-1805
(trimmed)
Gouache, 18.3 x 13 cm

tower

bread

Jan Steen
Leiden Baker Arent Oostwaard and His Wife Catharina Keizerswaard, 1658
(trimmed)
Oil on panel, 37.7 x 31.5 cm

balloon

G. Carbentus

The Launch of Blanchard's Balloon, The Hague, 1785
(trimmed)
Pencil, pen and grey ink, and watercolour, 35.2 x 46.2 cm

dragon

Yashima Gakutei
Woman on a Dragon, 1820
(trimmed)
Nishiki-e, 24 x 17.3 cm

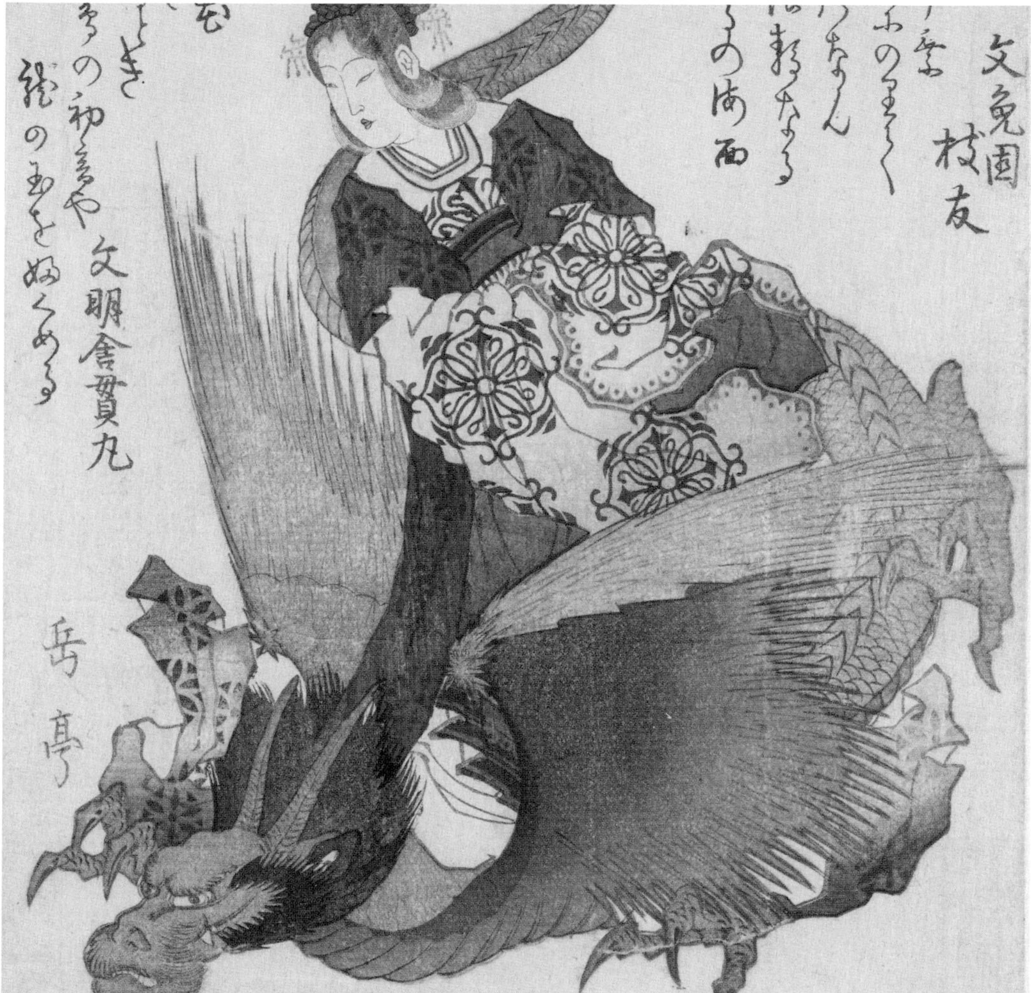
文兎園 枝友
岳亭

windmill

Paul Joseph Constantin Gabriël
'In the Month of July': a Windmill on a Polder Waterway, c. 1889
(trimmed)
Oil on canvas, 102 x 66 cm

fruit

Jacobus Linthorst
Still Life with Fruit, 1808
(trimmed)
Oil on panel, 84 x 66 cm

shell

Maria Sibylla Merian
A Tulip, Two Branches of Myrtle and Two Shells, c. 1657-1717
(detail)
Gouache on parchment, 33.6 x 24 cm

candle

Gerard Dou
The Nightschool, c. 1660-65
(detail)
Oil on panel, 74 x 64 cm

painting

tulip

Anonymous
Glass with a Tulip and Insect
(trimmed)
Grisaille on glass, 12 x 7.8 cm

legs

Jozef Israëls
David's Legs, 1899
(trimmed)
Oil on canvas, 47 x 34 cm

violin

dancers

David Teniers
Country Kermis, c. 1665
(detail)
Oil on canvas, 78 x 106.5 cm

castle

Claes Jacobsz. van der Heck
View of the Castle of Egmond aan den Hoef, c. 1638
(detail)
Oil on panel, 32.5 x 72.5 cm

lion

face

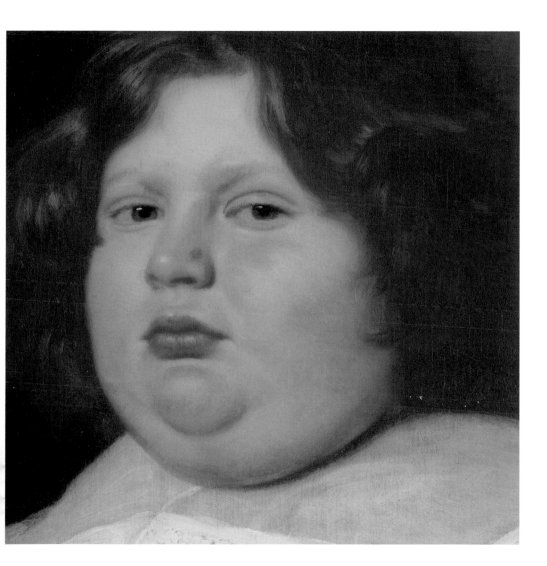

stairs

cactus

crown

Edwaert Collier
Vanitas Still Life, 1662
(detail)
Oil on canvas, 102.5 x 132 cm

flowers

Jan Toorop
Portrait of Marie Jeannette de Lange, 1900
(detail)
Oil on canvas, 70.5 x 77.4 cm

handkerchief

turtles

After a design of Nakamura Hochu
Three Turtles, 1826
(trimmed)
Coloured woodcut, 25.6 x 36.8 cm

roof

beard

Vincent van Gogh
Self Portrait, 1887
(detail)
Oil on cardboard, 42 x 34 cm

[80]

soldier

donkeys

Isaac Israels
Two Donkeys, c. 1897-1901
(trimmed)
Oil on cardboard, 46 x 61 cm

ice

hand

Charles Howard Hodges
Study of a Man's Hand Resting on White Fabric, c. 1774-1837
(trimmed)
Pastel on blue paper, 17.5 x 23.3 cm

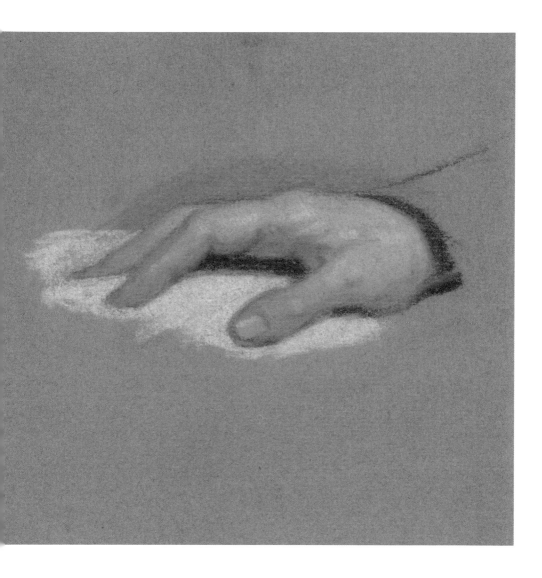

turban

Rembrandt
An Oriental, 1635
(trimmed)
Oil on panel, 72 x 54.5 cm

monkey

Hendrick Goltzius
A Chained Monkey, Seated, c. 1592-1602
(trimmed)
Black and coloured chalks, 40.6 x 30 cm

stocking

Jan Steen
Woman at Her Toilet, c. 1655-60
(trimmed)
Oil on panel, 37 x 27.5 cm

canal

Gerrit Adriaensz. Berckheyde
The Bend in the Herengracht, Amsterdam, 1671-72
(trimmed)
Oil on panel, 42.5 x 57.9 cm

cats

Henriëtte Ronner
The Harmonists, 1876-77
(trimmed)
Watercolour, 34.3 x 45.4 cm

milk

Johannes Vermeer
The Kitchen Maid, 1660
(trimmed)
Oil on canvas, 45.5 x 41 cm

bridge

Johan Hendrik Weissenbruch
Lift Bridge near Noorden, c. 1890
(trimmed)
Watercolour, 54.3 x 74 cm

giraffe

.

shop

Isaac Israels
A Shop Window, c. 1894-98
(trimmed)
Oil on canvas, 59 x 64 cm

egret

forest

Jacob Olie Jr.
Vivi in a Forest, c. 1910-27
(trimmed)
Photograph, 8.9 x 11.9 cm

book

Rembrandt
The Prophetess Anna (known as 'Rembrandt's Mother'), 1631
(detail)
Oil on panel, 60 x 48 cm

boy

farm

Johan Hendrik Weissenbruch
Peasant Cottage on a Waterway, c. 1870-1903
(trimmed)
Oil on panel, 17.5 x 24 cm

snow

Willem Witsen
Winter Landscape, c. 1885-1922
(trimmed)
Oil on canvas, 45 x 52 cm

dress

Gerard ter Borch
The Paternal Admonition, c. 1653-55
(trimmed)
Oil on canvas, 71 x 73 cm

waterfall

Abraham Teerlink
The Cascatelle near Tivoli, 1824
(detail)
Oil on canvas, 101.5 x 143 cm

zebra

Robert Jacob Gordon
Cape Mountain Zebra, c. 1777-86
(trimmed)
Pencil, pen and ink, watercolour and bodycolour, 22 x 37.1 cm

flute

Govert Flinck
Rembrandt as Shepherd with Staff and Flute, 1636
(trimmed)
Oil on canvas, 74.5 x 64 cm

bench

Aert Schouman
The Hamlet, De Lindt, in the Zwijndrechtse Waard near Meerdervoort, 1742
(detail)
Watercolour, 14 x 25.4 cm

lemon

skeleton

Jacob Joseph Eeckhout
Portrait of Frederik, Prince of Orange-Nassau, c. 1831-33
(detail)
Pencil and brush, 19.4 x 13.8

beak

Aert Schouman
Red-billed Toucan, 1748
(trimmed)
Watercolour, 48.2 x 31.9 cm

stick

Aelbert Cuyp
**A Senior Merchant of The Dutch East India Company,
Presumably Jacob Mathieusen, and His Wife,** c. 1640-60
(trimmed)
Oil on canvas, 138 x 208 cm

feet

Hendrick Goltzius
Dying Adonis, 1609
(detail)
Oil on canvas, 76.5 x 76.5 cm

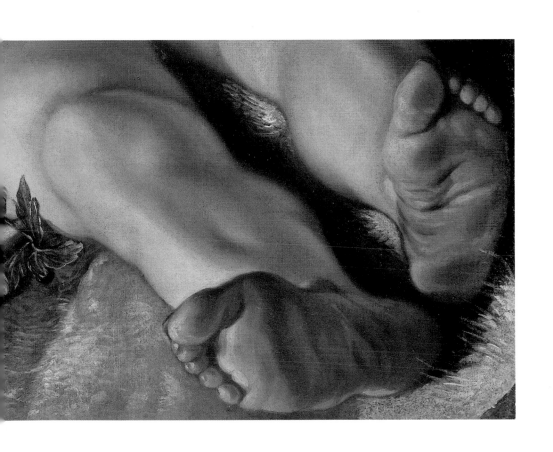

birds

Anonymous
Birds, Twigs and Fruits, c. 1750-1800
(trimmed)
Reliefprint, 31.3 x 37.3 cm

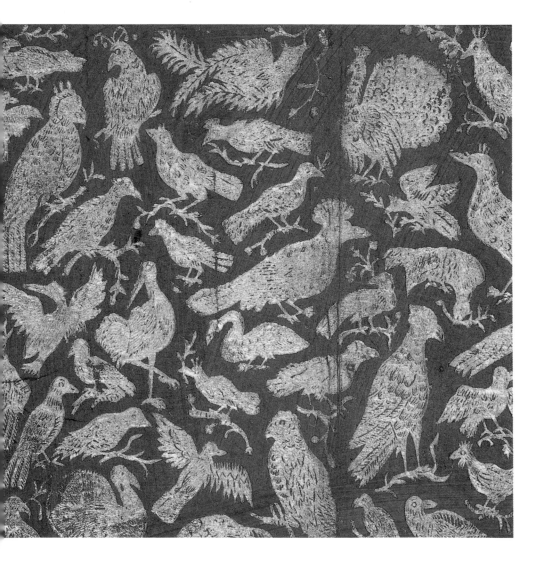

town hall

Gerrit Adriaensz. Berckheyde
The Town Hall on the Dam, Amsterdam, 1672
(trimmed)
Oil on canvas, 33.5 x 41.5 cm

room

Jacobus Ludovicus Cornet
The Room of Cornelis de Witt in Prison De Gevangenpoort, The Hague, 1844
(trimmed)
Chalk, pen and brush, 25.4 x 35.3 cm

wave

After a design of Katsushika Hokusai
The Underwave Off Kanagawa, c. 1829-33
(trimmed)
Coloured woodcut, 25.4 x 37.5 cm

ship

owl

Cornelis Cornelisz. van Haarlem
The Fall of Man, 1592
(detail)
Oil on canvas, 273 x 220 cm

berries

horse

Anthony Oberman
Adriaan van der Hoop's Trotter 'De Vlugge' in the Pasture, 1828
(trimmed)
Oil on canvas, 60 x 54 cm

boots

Rembrandt
Nightwatch, 1642
(detail)
Oil on canvas, 379.5 x 453.5 cm

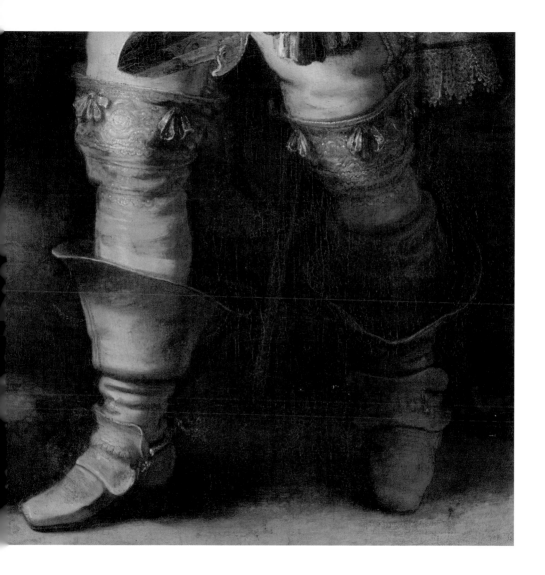

fur hat

Abraham van Strij
Man with Fur Hat and Pipe, c. 1763-1826
(trimmed)
Watercolour, 22.8 x 16.8 cm

ostrich

moon

Hendrick Avercamp
Fishermen by Moonlight, c. 1595-1634
(trimmed)
Pen and brown and black ink, with bodycolour, 14.4 x 19.5 cm

kimono

George Hendrik Breitner
Girl in a White Kimono, 1894
(trimmed)
Oil on canvas, 59 x 57 cm

glass

ducks

street

Johan Barthold Jongkind
Rue Notre-Dame, Paris, 1866
(trimmed)
Oil on canvas, 39 x 47 cm

king

clouds

Jacob Isaacksz. van Ruisdael
View of Haarlem, c. 1650-82
(trimmed)
Oil on canvas, 43 x 38 cm

dog

Attributed to Nicolas Toussaint Charlet
Head of a Dog, c. 1820-45
(trimmed)
Oil on canvas, 35 x 35 cm

smile

sea

Jan Toorop
The Sea, 1887
(trimmed)
Oil on canvas, 86 x 96 cm

bowl

Master of the Amsterdam Bodegón
Kitchen Scene (bodegón), c. 1610-25
(detail)
Oil on canvas, 100 x 122 cm

flag

H.Th. Hesselaar
A Factory on Java, 1851
(detail)
Oil on panel, 43 x 54 cm

swan

Jan Asselijn
The Threatened Swan, c. 1640-52
(trimmed)
Oil on canvas, 144 x 171 cm

rainbow

Jacob Cats
Autumn Landscape with Rainbow, 1797
(trimmed)
Watercolour and ink, 33.5 x 41.5 cm

hat

Caesar Boëtius van Everdingen
Young Woman in a Broad-Brimmed Hat, c. 1645-50
(trimmed)
Oil on canvas, 92.2 x 81.7 cm

bottles

cheese

Floris Claesz. van Dijck
Still Life with Cheeses, c. 1615
(detail)
Oil on panel, 82.2 x 111.2 cm

blossom

Geo Poggenbeek
An Orchard in Bloom, c. 1873-1903
(trimmed)
Oil on canvas on panel, 18.5 x 23.5 cm

artist

Hendrikus van de Sande Bakhuyzen
The Artist Painting a Cow in a Meadow Landscape, 1850
(detail)
Oil on panel, 73.2 x 96.7 cm

COWS

Paulus Potter
Four Cows in a Meadow, 1651
(trimmed)
Oil on panel, 25 x 30 cm

card

Johannes van Wijckersloot
Playing Cards over the Cradle, c. 1643-83
(trimmed)
Oil on canvas, 98 x 121 cm

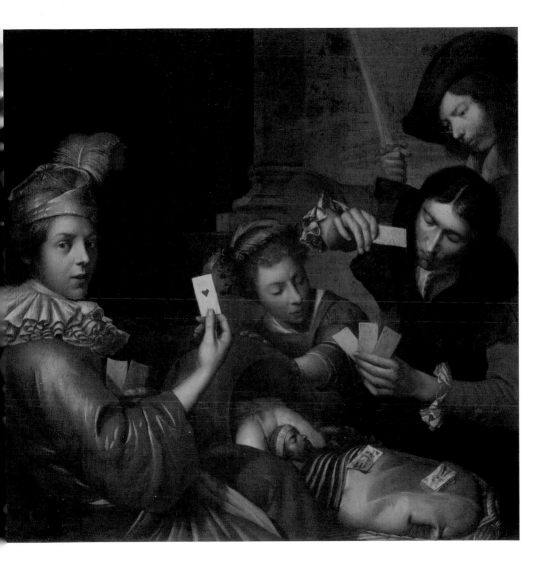

back

couple

Jozef Israëls
Jewish Wedding, 1903
(trimmed)
Oil on canvas, 137 x 148 cm

ditch

angel

Adriaen van de Velde
The Annunciation, 1667
(detail)
Oil on canvas, 128 x 176 cm

beetle

Jan Augustin van der Goes
Beetle, c. 1690-1700
(trimmed)
Gouache on parchment, 4.8 x 5.5 cm

[212]

doll's house

nose

coach

windows

baby

butterfly

Balthasar van der Ast
Still Life with Fruit and Flowers, 1620-21
(detail)
Oil on panel, 39.2 x 69.8 cm

ice-skaters

Adriaen Pietersz. van de Venne
Winter, 1625
(trimmed)
Oil on panel, 14.6 x 37.1

palms

Andries Beeckman
The Castle of Batavia, 1656-57
(trimmed)
Oil on canvas, 108 x 151.5 cm

beach

ruff

Werner van den Valckert
Portrait of a Man with Ring and Touchstone, 1617
(trimmed)
Oil on panel, 66 x 49.5 cm

fish

Willem Witsen
Side-view of a Fish, 1883
(trimmed)
Watercolour and chalk, 14.1 x 21 cm

cage

hill

Jan Brandes
Antropomorphic Hill, 1785
(trimmed)
Watercolour, 19.5 x 15.5 cm

[238]

bicycle

George Hendrik Breitner
Cyclist on the Prinsengracht, Amsterdam, c. 1890-1910
(trimmed)
Photograph, 40 x 27.4 cm

guitar

Louis de Carmontelle
Portrait of Madame de Montainville, Playing the Guitar, 1758
(trimmed)
Watercolour, 25.6 x 17.7 cm

apples

Gustave Courbet
Still Life with Apples, 1872
(trimmed)
Oil on canvas, 59 x 48 cm

church

Jan Abrahamsz. Beerstraten
View of the Church of Sloten in the Winter, c. 1640-66
(detail)
Oil on canvas, 90 x 128 cm

strawberry

Elisabeth Geertruida van de Kasteele
Strawberry, c. 1700-1800
(trimmed)
Watercolour, 10.6 x 11.2 cm

river

Kasparus Karsen
Imaginary View on the Rhine, c. 1840-70
(trimmed)
Oil on panel, 37 x 48.5 cm

[250]

elephant

kiss

Workshop of Quinten Massijs
Madonna and Child, c. 1525-30
(detail)
Oil on panel, 75.4 x 62.9 cm

About the artworks

www.queridokinderboeken.nl
www.rijksmuseum.nl

Compiled by Dik Zweekhorst, with thanks to Wieneke 't Hoen,
and to Martijn Pronk and Marieke de Jong at the Rijksmuseum

Cover artwork Brigitte Slangen
Design and layout Studio Cursief, Irma Hornman
Cover illustration (Anonymous) Portrait of William George Frederik, Prince of Orange-Nassau

ISBN 978 90 451 1499 6 / NUR 217